There's None So Blind

A play

Gillian Plowman

Samuel French—London
New York-Toronto-Hollywood

THERE'S NONE SO BLIND

First performed by Flat Four with the following cast:

Nicola	Frances Iles
Geoffrey	David Flint
Anton	Christopher Bartle
Alice	Gillian Plowman
Amaryllis	Karrie Stark
Peter	Daryl Bennett
Pietro	Robert Iles

Directed by Iris Bartle

CHARACTERS

Nicola, attractive, stylish; 30/40
Geoffrey, blind, well-built; 40s
Anton, active, false legs; late 40s
Alice, athletic, competent; 40s
Amaryllis, healthy, buxom; 30s
Peter, slim, handsome; 20s
Pietro, very well-built: balding; 40s

The action of the play takes place in Geoffrey's treatment room and the reception area of a leisure centre

Time — the present

*Other plays by Gillian Plowman
published by Samuel French Ltd:*

Beata Beatrix
Cecily
Close to Croydon
David's Birthday
The Janna Years
A Kind of Vesuvius
Me and My Friend
Philip and Rowena
Tippers
Two Summers
Unjama Land

THERE'S NONE SO BLIND

The treatment room where Geoffrey works as a reflexologist

In the room there are: a chair with an extending footrest, set in a reclining position and covered with a cosy white towel or similar; a low stool at the foot of the chair; a desk with a computer, dictaphone, telephone, CD remote control and diary on it, with a typing chair; and plants

The Lights come up. Geoffrey and Nicola are on stage. Nicola is an attractive, stylish woman, aged thirty to forty; Geoffrey is well-built, blind, and in his forties. Nicola has obviously just entered the room. She bursts into speech

Nicola One more lorry. I said to him, one more lorry and I go. And he said how am I going and where am I going and the business is expanding and we're rich and a house in the Bahamas is in the offing and why don't I just stop wittering about pollution and reap the benefits of all our hard work. More methane is produced by sheep farting in New Zealand, he said, than a million lorries. Sheep can't help farting in New Zealand. We don't need another lorry.

Geoffrey He's a very astute businessman, your husband.

Nicola Geoffrey, people can't *breathe*.

Geoffrey Come. Come and sit down. Take your shoes off.

Nicola takes off her jacket, slips her shoes off and sits on the relaxing chair

Nicola I've washed them.

Geoffrey You always do. So many stresses, locked into your body.

Geoffrey works on Nicola's feet during the following

Nicola He thinks *this* is stupid — reflexology. Says how can twiddling your toes cure asthma?

Geoffrey It can.

Nicola I know it can.

Geoffrey By working on the tiny deposits and imbalances in the feet we can release blockages and restore the free flow of energy to the whole body.

Nicola When I'm here, I can feel that flow of energy — starting — moving through me.

Geoffrey Good.

Nicola When I'm not here, my life is blocked again.

Geoffrey Not if we keep working at it. (*He works for a moment*) A house in the Bahamas sounds very relaxing — for the sake of one more lorry ...

Nicola A lorry that will release its own weight in carbon into the atmosphere every *year*! (*Beat*) I get on his nerves — all this pollution business. (*Beat*) He'll leave me.

Geoffrey Do you think so?

Nicola Inevitably.

Geoffrey Surely not. You're partners, in all senses.

Nicola Not equal. In any sense. There's always one who loves more than the other. Don't you think?

Geoffrey The business, though.

Nicola He has fifty-one per cent of the company.

Geoffrey And you have forty-nine.

Nicola I'm not sure how many lorries that is. He'd have to buy me out.

Geoffrey I'm sure it won't come to that. (*He works for a moment. Jokingly*) Though if it does, you make sure you strike a very hard bargain!

Nicola laughs slightly

Nicola Your wife ...
Geoffrey Alice.

Nicola Yes. Do you get on her nerves?

Geoffrey She's very fit. She gets cross with me because I don't do enough exercise. Hates me being overweight. Holds my hand and takes me out jogging. I hate jogging. (*He shudders*)

Nicola Who loves the most?

Beat

Geoffrey Mmm.

Beat

Nicola The other thing that gets on his nerves — I can't pass my driving test! Can you imagine? In our business. He can't believe my lack of spatial awareness.

Geoffrey Health is our business. She can't believe my lack of will power.

Geoffrey continues with Nicola's feet. She cries out in pain

That's the place. (*He works on it*) The pain will ease.

Beat

Nicola Your eyes.

Geoffrey My eyes.

Nicola Why do you think God gave you eyes that don't work? Gave me lungs that can't breathe?

Geoffrey Everybody I meet is thankful they can see.

Nicola Can't have a world without "Thank God". Thank God it's not me who can't see. Thank God it's not me who can't breathe.

Geoffrey So there's a reason ——

Nicola Yes! Wants us praying endlessly for things we can't have.

Geoffrey Three deep breaths. In. Out. In. Out. In. Out.

Nicola breathes deeply

There you are. How easy it was. Maybe there are things we can have.

Nicola If we work at it.
Geoffrey Together, Nicola.

Nicola sits up

There is a knock at the door

Anton (*off*) Geoffrey, can I come in?
Nicola It's all right. (*She puts her jacket on*)
Geoffrey Come in, Anton.

Anton enters, carrying a box. Anton is in his late forties, an active-looking man with false legs

Anton Oh, sorry.
Nicola I'm just going.
Anton Ah.
Nicola You having your feet done?
Anton No feet.
Nicola No feet?
Anton Blown off.
Nicola Oh!
Anton Can't do reflexology on a pair of tin plates.
Nicola (*to Geoffrey*) You see! "Thank God!" "Thank God!"
Anton Exactly. Thank God for an excuse not to have reflexology.
Geoffrey Anton's my marketing manager.
Anton No, I'm not.
Nicola I can't come for a while.
Geoffrey Good, isn't he?
Nicola Till next Thursday.
Geoffrey Have a look.

Nicola checks the diary and writes herself in

Nicola Half-past four Thursday.
Geoffrey Nicola, visualize a sunset.

Nicola That's all very well for you to say. Tomorrow, we're going to Germany to buy a new lorry!

Nicola exits

Anton looks at Geoffrey

Geoffrey Are you looking at me?
Anton Yes.
Geoffrey Quizzically?
Anton Yes.
Geoffrey Can't say anything.
Anton Visualize a sunset?
Geoffrey Or dance. Both good for stress.
Anton On your own?
Geoffrey Can do.
Anton Hey! *Dancing in the Dark* — your theme tune!
Geoffrey "Dance Till Your Legs Drop Off". Yours.
Anton No such song.
Geoffrey What do you want anyway?
Anton Look. (*He opens his box and gets out some roller-skate wheels*)
Geoffrey I'm looking.
Anton Geoffrey.
Geoffrey Anton.
Anton You're always trying to trip me up!

They laugh

Geoffrey I'm looking at … ?
Anton Wheels.
Geoffrey Wheels? Ferris wheels? Bicycle wheels? Or has someone given you a jolly good whipping and you've got streaks on your flesh?
Anton I wish.
Geoffrey Now it's all coming out.

Anton Don't you have fantasies?

Geoffrey One of them's having a new next-door neighbour, Anton.

Anton Funny. I have that one too.

Geoffrey All right, what are these wheels for?

Anton My tin plates.

Anton hands the wheels to Geoffrey

Geoffrey You're going to fix these wheels on to your tin plates?

Anton You know how slow our walks have become?

Geoffrey I don't mind. I like slow.

Anton Alice likes fast.

Geoffrey Alice doesn't come on our walks.

Anton Alice wants slim.

Geoffrey Why are you on Alice's side suddenly?

Anton I'm not. Both of you. You're … I envy you. You and Alice. What you've got.

Geoffrey Am I letting myself go, Anton? Is that what you're saying?

Anton It's not what I'm saying.

Geoffrey I'm putting on weight.

Anton That's not what I'm saying.

Geoffrey I hear what you're saying. I may not be able to see into a mirror but I do care what I look like. Have I got blackheads? Are my teeth becoming stained?

Anton *That's* not what I'm saying. Oh, for goodness' sake, let's go out and have some fun. Have we had a lot of fun lately?

Geoffrey Yes. Chelsea keep winning.

Anton That's not us doing that.

Geoffrey It bloody is! You describe the match for me and I jump up and down for you! That's us, doing that.

Anton This is the same thing.

Geoffrey What is?

Anton I'll wear the wheels and you push me and we'll have fun and exercise and get there faster all in one go.

Geoffrey Where?

Anton Pub?

Pause

Geoffrey What? Anton?
Anton I can't.
Geoffrey What?
Anton Put them on.
Geoffrey Why not? Don't they fit?
Anton I can't.
Geoffrey Frightened?

Silence

   I would be too. Putting on a pair of roller-skates. Can you
   imagine? The two of us on wheels? Terrifying.
Anton For everyone else on the street!
Geoffrey Absolutely. (*Beat*) We go on about it, don't we. Don't
   treat us differently. We are not disabled. We're absolutely normal.
   We may have a disability or two — provide for us. But don't treat
   us differently. (*Beat*) But we are different, Anton. You and me.
   We're terrified of putting on a pair of roller-skates.
Anton You're more normal than I am.
Geoffrey I'm more terrified.
Anton You've got Alice. She makes your life normal.
Geoffrey Why did you never marry?
Anton Never met my ideal woman.
Geoffrey And she is?
Anton She's big, she's jolly, she can lift me off my feet, and out of
   my depressions. She's got tits like melons and a rear like the Ark
   Royal. She's got thighs like iron and a heart as soft as cotton wool.
   (*Beat*) My legs make no difference to her. (*Beat*) She loves me.
   She makes my life normal.
Geoffrey We'll find her.
Anton I doubt it.
Geoffrey Keep looking.
Anton And you.
Geoffrey Yeh, I'll keep looking.
Anton Arsehole!

Geoffrey Advertise. WLTM — would like to meet — TLM — tits
   like melons …
Anton Get arrested.
Geoffrey Walk to the pub then?
Anton (*looking at his wheels*) I had courage once.
Geoffrey You still have, matey-boy. You still have. Walking to the
   pub. That's courage.

Geoffrey and Anton exit L

Alice enters R. *She is a trim woman in a track suit. She carries a
shopping bag and some unopened letters. She puts the letters on
the desk*

Alice (*calling*) Geoffrey!

Alice exits into the kitchen and returns without her shopping bag

(*Picking up the diary and turning to the following day's date, then
picking up the dictaphone and talking into it*) Appointments for
Tuesday sixteenth — that's tomorrow, Geoffrey — start at ten
a.m. with Mr Cousins. Eleven-thirty Danniella McIlroy. Then no-
one till three in the afternoon. I'll come home in my lunch hour
and pick you up for a swim. Don't moan. It's disabled swimming
from one till two — the pool will be nearly empty. (*She rewinds
the tape for a moment and re-records the last part of the message*)
It's reserved swimming from one till two — the pool won't be at
all crowded. I'll get you back for your three o'clock appointment.
(*She stops the tape, then starts again*) I've had to go straight back
to the leisure centre. Sorry. Somebody's off sick. I'll eat there,
don't worry. Got your salad dressing. On right of sink, next to
spring onions. Back about ten. Love you. (*She re-winds the tape
to eliminate the last five words*) Back about ten. (*She stops there,
then starts again*) Lunchtime post. Gas bill. Electricity bill. Card
from my garage saying the MOT's due. Letter from Sarah! I'll
take it with me to read. And a letter for you. Local. I'll read it when
I get back. I know that's three shifts in one day. Don't miss me too
much! (*She puts the overseas letter from Sarah in her bag, leaving*

the others) Alice. (*She switches off the dictaphone, rewinds the tape and puts the machine on the desk*)

Alice exits

The Lights fade to an evening setting, with a mellow light and the glow from the computer screen. Music fades in: Let's Face the Music and Dance

Geoffrey enters and dances by himself, slowly and sadly, with tears in his eyes

Alice (*off*) Geoffrey!

Geoffrey wipes his face, sits at the desk and switches off the music with the remote control

Alice enters with her handbag. She switches on the main light

You're in the dark again.
Geoffrey My contribution to the electricity bill.
Alice We'll get burglars.
Geoffrey Why will we?
Alice If the house is always in the dark. They'll think it's empty.
Geoffrey They'll find me here.
Alice Yes, and they'll probably beat you up.
Geoffrey Will that matter?

Alice looks at him

Alice Have you eaten?
Geoffrey No. I'm losing weight.
Alice Not eating won't help you lose weight.
Geoffrey 'Course it will. There were no fat people in Belsen.
Alice Little and often of the right sort of food. Otherwise Mother Nature will think there's a famine on and lay down stores of fat.

Alice touches Geoffrey's tummy but he freezes unresponsively

Are you all right?

Geoffrey Mmm.

Alice Your hair's thinning, Geoffrey.

Geoffrey Is it?

Alice I'll crack an egg on it if you like. Give it plenty of protein. Massage it in.

Alice works her fingers through Geoffrey's hair. He is still unresponsive. Alice backs off and gets Sarah's letter out of her bag

Sarah's letter. Shall I read it?

No reply

(*Reading*) "Dear Mum and Dad. Made it to Vic Falls after two weeks in Namibia and Botswana on our tour bus which was good fun. Namibia was beautiful, especially the red sand dunes of the Namib desert, and the wildlife of course. We also went on an overnight trip in the Okanango delta in Botswana by traditional wooden canoe which was excellent also. The Falls were a bit dry but still very impressive and the best time for white water rafting which was amazing — a real adventure buzz. Now I'm in Bulawayo at the start of the next part of the journey up to Nairobi. Went to a park today on a day tour and got really close on foot to rhinos in the wild. Oh — saw lions in Namibia and buffalo in Okanango so only need leopards now for so-called Big Five (elephants are easiest — they're everywhere). Hope you're both well. All my love, Sarah."

Geoffrey You could have left it.

Alice What?

Geoffrey Sarah's letter. You didn't have to take it with you.

Alice I wanted to read it.

Geoffrey I wanted to read it.

Alice Well, you can't.

Geoffrey Anton was here.

Alice He's not reading my daughter's letter before me.

Geoffrey *He* wouldn't have been reading it. He would have been reading it to *me*. I would have been reading it.

Alice What if she'd said something personal in it?

Geoffrey Of course she would have said something personal in it. It's from her, personally.

Alice What if she was pregnant?

Geoffrey Is she pregnant?

Alice I've just read you the letter. She's not pregnant.

Geoffrey You might have left that bit out.

Alice Why would I leave that bit out?

Geoffrey To keep it from me.

Alice I've spent twenty-five years telling you things, Geoffrey. I don't leave things out. Sometimes I feel like an information bureau. I feel like closing sometimes, Geoffrey.

Beat

Sorry. I've had a long day.

Geoffrey Three shifts.

Alice Yes.

Geoffrey You tell me everything, do you?

Alice Yes.

Geoffrey About your work?

Alice I don't tell you everything about my work.

Geoffrey Why not?

Alice You don't tell me everything about yours.

Geoffrey It's here. My work is here. You have access to it.

Alice I don't know what — you say to a client.

Geoffrey It's on the computer.

Alice You could be leaving things out! What's this all about Geoffrey?

Geoffrey I don't know what goes on at the leisure centre.

Alice Sport, mainly.

Geoffrey I bet.

Alice It's hard work, telling you everything ... It would be like doing another shift ——

Geoffrey You haven't told me about Peter Clemenson.

Beat

There was a sharp intake of breath on your part, Alice.

Alice What about Peter Clemenson?
Geoffrey You were going to read this letter for me when you came
  home.

Geoffrey hands Alice a letter from the lunchtime post

Alice It's open.
Geoffrey Yes.
Alice Who's it from?
Geoffrey Read it and see.

Alice takes the letter out of the envelope and reads it. She gasps

  Another sharp intake of breath there, Alice. (*Beat*) Read it to me
  then.
Alice You know what it says.
Geoffrey Read it.
Alice "Dear Geoffrey Holbourne."

Pause

Geoffrey Spelt correctly. People usually get one or the other wrong.
Alice Who would write … ?
Geoffrey Somebody who knows.
Alice What?
Geoffrey Read it!
Alice (*reading*) "I've never written a letter like this before, but I
  can't stand by and let her get away with it. I know that you can't
  see. You can't see what's going on between your wife and another
  member of staff at the leisure centre … " Geoffrey, for goodness'
  sake!
Geoffrey What? For goodness' sake, what, Alice?

Silence

  Read it!
Alice (*reading*) "She is having an affair with Peter Clemenson.

Please believe that this comes not from a trouble-maker, but from one who cares about fair play." That's all.

Geoffrey (*shouting*) "That's all"?

Alice That's all that's in the letter. I suppose Anton read this?

Geoffrey Is it true?

Alice Did he?

Geoffrey Is it?

Alice I don't know.

Geoffrey You don't know!

Alice But everybody else will, if Anton has anything to do with it. The whole bloody street. Nice bit of gossip. I don't want people reading our letters.

Geoffrey My letter. That was my letter.

Alice About me.

Geoffrey About you and Peter Clemenson.

Pause

This moment, Alice, is like the moment of conception when everything seems the same but the whole of life changes. I need this moment to be precise.

Alice This moment is about me as well.

Geoffrey Then be precise.

Alice I like Peter.

Geoffrey Of course you like him! You're having an affair with him.

Alice What does that mean?

Geoffrey You tell me.

Alice I like him …

Geoffrey You said.

Alice He makes me laugh. I'm attracted to him. I didn't mean to be. It was — you know — a good working relationship. Supportive …

Geoffrey Why do you need supporting. Because you have to look after a blind husband?

Alice Because of pressures at work …

Geoffrey You lied, didn't you? Late evenings. Extra shifts.

Alice Sometimes, yes. I have been working hard …

Geoffrey Working hard. On what? Adultery?

Alice Doing my job. On my promotion.

Geoffrey How many people do you have to sleep with to get promoted?

Alice You wanted precise.

Geoffrey Precisely how many people do you have to sleep with to get promoted?

Alice I'm going to bed. (*She turns to go*)

Geoffrey moves to stop Alice; he knows the room so well he can do this. There are clumsy moments and physical clashes

Geoffrey Fucking well stay here!

Alice You won't listen.

Geoffrey stops moving

Geoffrey I'll listen.

Alice You've been crying.

Geoffrey One way they work.

Pause

Alice I don't know which truth would hurt the most.

Pause

If I said, "Yes, I was sleeping with Peter — an affair — I'm sorry you had to find out, but that's all it is", you'd be hurt.

Pause

If I said, "No, I haven't, yet — but I want to. (*Beat*) If I sleep with him, I couldn't turn back. (*Beat*) I would go to him." (*Beat*) Does that hurt more or less?

Geoffrey (*after a beat; quiet in his pain*) Which is it?

Alice I'm not going to him.

Geoffrey Why not?

Alice How can I?

Geoffrey Doesn't he want you?

Alice Yes.

Geoffrey Is he putting his wife through this? Now? This minute?

Alice She died.

Geoffrey So he gets the sympathy vote. What's stopping you?

Alice Geoffrey …

Geoffrey What?

Alice I can't leave you.

Geoffrey You can. Fuck off.

Alice Don't.

Geoffrey He's free. He wants you. You want him. You're free. Feel free.

Alice This is ridiculous.

Geoffrey What is.

Alice You … need me, Geoffrey.

Geoffrey Oh, that's it, is it? You can't leave me because I can't manage without you. I can't see without you? Run my business without you? Keep in touch with my daughter without you? *Exist* without you? (*Beat*) I will not be treated as someone you can't leave.

Alice Well you are someone I can't leave.

Geoffrey Because you'd have a guilty conscience? Because people would point the finger at the heartless cow who left her blind husband for an all-seeing, all-dancing leisure centre gigolo. If you want Peter Clemenson, Alice, then have the courage of your convictions and bugger off.

Alice I haven't decided.

Geoffrey It's decided.

Alice Stop telling me what to do.

Geoffrey Makes a change from the other way round. I suppose he's young, slim, worked out and hot-blooded. Won't need any describing, Alice. Won't need to sit obediently whilst eggs are broken over his head. You'll be able to concentrate on athletic pursuits like sex.

Alice It's not … Sex isn't … It's not about sex …

Geoffrey Kissing is having sex, Alice. Holding hands. Sitting so
close that the whole lengths of your legs are touching. Have you
done that, Alice?

No reply

How long, Alice, how long have I been making love to you and
you've been thinking of him? Knowing that I cannot see your
face, have you been looking at him?

Alice This stupid letter … I don't know … Maybe it would just have
gone away …

Geoffrey And I'd never have known?

Alice It's not …

Geoffrey Go to him.

Alice (*turning to leave*) I can't.

Geoffrey I'm making it easy for you.

Alice You're making it impossible.

Alice exits

The Lights fade

*The set is changed to the reception area of a leisure centre. The
reflexology chair is set upright and the cover is removed. The desk
and computer remain in their former positions. A clipboard is
placed on the desk*

The Lights come up on a different setting from that used previously

*Amaryllis Hockthorne-Hunter enters in aerobics kit. She is in her
thirties and is everything Anton described as his ideal woman,
buxom and fit-looking*

Amaryllis Peter!

The phone rings. There is no-one to answer it so Amaryllis does so

(*Into the phone*) Squash court tomorrow, five-thirty. Can do. ...
Have you got booking rights? ... Card number? (*She taps the
number into the computer*) HS/30402. ... Derry, it's you. Why
didn't you say? ... It's Amaryllis. ... Oh full bloom, darling, full
bloom. And yourself?

*Peter enters in aerobics kit. He is a slim, handsome man in his
twenties*

(*To Peter*) Peter! (*She points to her clipboard*)

Peter picks up the clipboard

(*Into the phone*) Listen, we've got a new professional men's
aerobics class started. Why don't you sign up? Do you good. ...
Oh all right. See you on the squash court then. ... How will I? I've
booked you the one with glass walls! (*She puts the phone down*)

Peter You know everyone, don't you?

Amaryllis Everyone a little and nobody a lot. Ah well.

Peter I'm so nervous.

Amaryllis You'll be fine. It's such a good innovation, this men's
class. You don't want to be a lifeguard all your life, do you?

Peter Do you think anyone will turn up?

Amaryllis It's only a small course to begin with, but it *will* catch
on. You'll see. They'll all want to look like you. And their wives
will all want them to look like you so they'll make them come.

Peter Wouldn't you be better for the men's class?

Amaryllis Wives don't seem to like me. They'd stop them coming.

*Anton and Geoffrey enter, Geoffrey using Anton's elbow for
guidance as he follows him in*

Looks like your class starting to arrive.

Peter Oh God, I need a glass of water.

Peter exits

Amaryllis moves to meet Anton and Geoffrey

Amaryllis Hallo. I'm Amaryllis Hockthorne-Hunter. Never gets shortened.

Anton is stunned by the sight of Amaryllis

   You're … ?
Anton Anton.
Amaryllis Anton something? (*She checks her clipboard but cannot find his name*)
Anton Babington-Smith.
Amaryllis A fellow hyphen. I hope you never get shortened. (*She adds his name to her list*)
Anton I was once.
Amaryllis Were you?
Anton By two feet.
Amaryllis (*not understanding*) Were you?

Pause; Amaryllis looks puzzled

   (*To Geoffrey*) And you are?
Geoffrey Me?
Amaryllis Yes, sorry.

Amaryllis reaches out and touches Geoffrey

   You are?
Geoffrey Geoffrey Holbourne.
Amaryllis Alice's husband!
Geoffrey Yes.
Amaryllis Lovely to meet you. I'm Amaryllis Hockthorne-Hunter. I expect you've heard about me. About everyone, I expect. (*She extends her hand*)
Anton Geoffrey, shake hands.

Amaryllis and Geoffrey shake hands

Amaryllis You come swimming sometimes, don't you?
Geoffrey I come swimming, yes.
Amaryllis And do *you* swim?
Anton No. I'd rust.

Pause; Amaryllis still doesn't understand

Amaryllis This is your first time in aerobics?
Geoffrey Anton, what are we doing in aerobics?
Amaryllis New idea. New class. Help keep us young and fit.
Anton We were told …
Geoffrey I want to see Peter Clemenson.
Amaryllis He's taking the class. Why don't you change whilst I go
    and chase him? (*She looks at her watch*)
Anton Change?
Amaryllis Track suit bottoms or something?
Anton We're in the aerobics class?
Amaryllis Aren't you?
Anton It's just … (*He taps his false legs*)

Amaryllis taps her own legs as a question

    False legs.
Amaryllis (*understanding now*) Honestly, you two are marvellous.
    Absolutely no reason why you shouldn't. I admire you.
Anton Really?
Amaryllis Absolutely.
Anton Really.
Amaryllis I guess Alice is the driving force behind Geoffrey
    coming. Isn't that right? Blind makes no difference, she says. And
    I expect your wife is just as encouraging, Anton?
Anton No wife.
Amaryllis No wife? (*Beat*) I'll go and get Peter.

Anton and Amaryllis smile at each other

    Amaryllis exits

Silence

Geoffrey Anton?

Anton decides not to tell Geoffrey at this moment that he has met his ideal woman

Anton Geoffrey.
Geoffrey I don't know what I'm doing here.
Anton You're going to tell Peter Clemenson to leave Alice alone. It's as simple as that.
Geoffrey Is it?
Anton You can hardly have a duel with him.
Geoffrey No.
Anton Just tell him, that's all.
Geoffrey Yes.

Peter and Amaryllis enter

Amaryllis Here we are.
Geoffrey What am I up against, Anton?
Anton I know what I'd like to be up against. (*Beat*) You're up against twenty-eight, tall, dark and handsome, slim as a whistle and with Rudolf Nureyev accoutrements.
Geoffrey Twenty-eight?
Anton Twenty-nine. Thirty.
Amaryllis No-one else arrived?
Geoffrey Any advance on thirty?

Peter does some bends

Anton Twenty-seven, twenty-six …
Geoffrey Twenty-six?
Amaryllis Extraordinary, isn't it? It's just Anton (*she points to her legs*) and Geoffrey (*she points to her eyes*), Peter.
Peter (*under his breath*) Oh my God!
Geoffrey He's a toy boy, Anton.

Anton Perhaps it's just a phase. It'll blow over.

Peter Hallo. I'm Peter. I'm really pleased that somebody's come. It's my first class … I *am* trained — and — I'm really pleased that you're — it. Right …

Anton He certainly hasn't got your wit and wisdom, Geoffrey.

Geoffrey starts moving towards Peter's voice

Amaryllis Put the music on then, Peter.

Peter (*aside to Amaryllis*) She's made them come, hasn't she?

Amaryllis Who?

Peter Alice.

Amaryllis Why would she do that?

Peter So that I'd have somebody in my class. To make me feel better.

Geoffrey Alice makes you feel better a lot, does she?

Peter Yes, she does.

Geoffrey reaches out and touches Peter

What are you doing?

Geoffrey Finding out what you look like.

Peter Oh.

Peter looks uncertainly at Amaryllis who looks uncertainly at Anton

Geoffrey You understand, Peter, that if you can't see things, you have to feel things.

Geoffrey feels Peter's face and body during the following

Peter Yes, I see.

Anton Geoffrey!

Peter It's all right.

Geoffrey Thank you for being so understanding.

Peter That's all right.

Geoffrey You do see, Anton, the advantages of being blind.

Anton looks at Amaryllis and away. During the following, Anton stands stiffly, very still

You are not influenced by physical appearance. You get a real sense of what a person's like without that barrier. (*Beat*) The real feeling of a person.

Peter Have you done enough feeling now?

Geoffrey Yes. You are beautiful.

Peter Well, you know — diet, exercise.

Geoffrey Now I know what you look like. Now I understand.

Peter What?

Geoffrey Why my wife fancies you.

Peter What!

Geoffrey You're having an affair with my wife.

Amaryllis Peter is?!

Peter I didn't know that.

Amaryllis Peter, you're not.

Geoffrey Alice has admitted it.

Peter No. Not an affair, no.

Geoffrey Are you saying she's lying?

Peter No of course not.

Geoffrey I believe you.

Peter Oh good.

Amaryllis You've only got to look at him to see he's telling the truth.

Anton He can't look at him.

Amaryllis Oh.

Geoffrey You're not sleeping with her, but you want to. If an affair is all in the mind, it's still an affair. But you can deny it. Because in truth it hasn't happened. Yet it has…

Peter Oh my giddy aunt. We've had a drink together but that was in the way of — well — work. A drink's not an affair, is it? Oh fuck.

Geoffrey Exactly.

Peter No, I didn't mean ——

Geoffrey Don't ever touch her again. Don't drink with her. Don't talk to her.

Peter She's my line manager.

Geoffrey She's my wife. One move in her direction and I'll kill you. I won't, of course. It's what you say to make you feel powerful when really you feel helpless.

Peter Yes.

Geoffrey You understand.

Peter Yes. I often feel helpless. I can't always think of something powerful to say. I never can.

Geoffrey Did you ever lose the woman you love to another man?

Pause

Amaryllis Peter's gay, Geoffrey.

Pause

Geoffrey Does Alice know?

Amaryllis Yes.

Geoffrey Poor Alice.

Amaryllis We're all happy about it.

Realization strikes Amaryllis and Peter

Peter My father!

Amaryllis Your father!

Geoffrey Your father?

Peter Oh no! My father's called Peter as well, you see.

Geoffrey And he's here?

Peter He's the catering manager.

Anton Amaryllis.

Amaryllis Yes?

Anton I'm not sure I'm cut out for aerobics.

Amaryllis Course you are. We're absolutely equal opportunities here. Whatever legs you've got.

Anton My legs have seized up.

Amaryllis I'll take them to the first aid room and do something about them.

Peter and Amaryllis pick Anton up

Anton Will you? How kind.
Geoffrey Peter Clemenson. Where will I find your father?
Peter I'll tell him.

   Peter, Anton and Amaryllis exit

The Lights fade

Two stools are set on stage

*The Lights come up on Geoffrey and Pietro — in his forties, balding
and very well built, in a cook's uniform — seated on the two stools*

Pietro I know, I know, it's very confusing. My father's called Peter
   too.
Geoffrey Does he work here?
Pietro No.
Geoffrey I got the wrong Peter Clemenson! I accused your son of
   having an affair with my wife. Can you imagine?

Pause

Pietro I can imagine, yes.
Geoffrey I feel very stupid.
Pietro You shouldn't. Perfectly understandable.
Geoffrey Thank you. So you're the catering manager.
Pietro Hands on.
Geoffrey I can imagine.

Pause

Pietro People call me Pietro.
Geoffrey Alice doesn't.
Pietro No, Alice doesn't.
Geoffrey Why are you called Pietro?

Pietro I'm famous for my pasta.

Geoffrey Your pasta?

Pietro (*kissing his fingers*) I spent several years in Naples learning to cook pasta.

Geoffrey Do you wish you were back there?

Pietro No. Do you?

Geoffrey I've never lived in Naples.

Pietro You deliberately misunderstand me.

Geoffrey I'm sorry. I want to do what's right. *Say* the right thing.

Pietro Yes.

Geoffrey I needed that affirmation. That you understand.

Pietro I do.

Geoffrey Are you tall?

Pietro Ish.

Geoffrey Trim?

Pietro Ish.

Geoffrey Mop of glossy hair?

Pietro Ish.

Geoffrey Do you crack eggs on it?

Pietro My hair?

Geoffrey Yes.

Pietro No.

Geoffrey And you run five miles before breakfast.

Pietro I don't.

Geoffrey After breakfast.

Pietro Surely that's the Greeks?

Geoffrey Olympics.

Pietro All that.

Geoffrey You're not Greek.

Pietro I'm not Italian.

Geoffrey But you're famous for your pasta.

Pietro My first love.

Geoffrey Not very flattering.

Pietro Who to?

Geoffrey Alice.

Pietro Oh.

Geoffrey My wife.

Pietro Yes.

Geoffrey Alice is more important to me than pasta.

Pietro Pasta with basil and walnut sauce?

Geoffrey Of course.

Pietro No. How can a woman be more important than food? Without food we weaken. Without food our emotions fade and our passions wither. Without food we can't have sex. Without food, woman has no significance.

Geoffrey You can live without pasta and basil and walnut sauce.

Pietro Have you tried it?

Geoffrey No.

Pietro Geoffrey. Come to supper tonight and I will make it for you.

Geoffrey I can't just come for supper tonight.

Pietro Why not?

Geoffrey Because of Alice.

Pietro Shall we invite her as well, or shall it just be the two of us?

Geoffrey How can you be so cavalier about Alice? She's the woman in your life. You're in love with her.

Pause

Pietro I'm sorry.

Geoffrey Why?

Pietro Another man's wife.

Geoffrey A blind man's wife?

Pause

She's not my wife.

Pietro (*surprised*) Isn't she?

Geoffrey I mean, she's Alice. Person in her own right.

Pietro Leisure Centre Manager.

Geoffrey Is she good at it?

Pietro Very. Motivates people.

Geoffrey Does she?

Pietro You must know that.

Geoffrey The trouble is, I've never thought of her like that. As a person in her own right. She is a part of me. She's my friend, my lover, my eyes. My diary. My world. Twenty-five years ago she said to me, "You know, you're very good-looking." And the dawn broke over my life. She married me. Can you imagine that. And she made it seem like *she* was the lucky one. (*Beat*) I brush her hair. (*Beat*) I smell her. Like a dog I follow her scent when she's not there. Stand in her places. (*Beat*) She makes me busy. Makes me work. Makes me swim. And I wait for her presence. (*Beat*) Sometimes we dance. We light candles. I can feel the candle-light. Her in the candle-light. (*Beat*) She is me. (*Beat*) It is astounding to know differently. Shocking. Life-threatening. To know that she is also somebody else. She is you. You have become part of her. Touched her. Laughed with her. (*Beat*) Twenty-five years later she says to me, "I would go to him."

Pietro She won't leave you.

Geoffrey Sleep with her but once and she will come to you.

Pietro She's made it very clear.

Pause

Geoffrey Is that not untenable for you? Knowing that this woman, for whom you feel such passion, cannot come to you?

Pietro Well, of course, I ... No. I'll survive.

Geoffrey Both of you longing to be together yet denying yourselves.

Pietro We're grown-up, Geoffrey. You can't just ...

Geoffrey Take what you want in life?

Pietro Destroy another person.

Geoffrey Me?

Pietro And Alice. She couldn't live with herself ...

Geoffrey I am destroyed!

Pietro No. Nothing will happen. Everything will stay as it is.

Geoffrey I can't un-know the knowledge that she is not me! We are split asunder. She can't stay. (*Beat*) I can't have her stay. (*Beat*) There is that moment when everything seems the same but the whole of life changes. (*Beat*) If she stayed, I would destroy her life. (*Beat*) Help me to save her!

Pause

Pietro The moment when Alice becomes more important than pasta.
Geoffrey Yes.
Pietro What would you have me do?
Geoffrey You know.
Pietro She's her own person.
Geoffrey Then it must be her decision.
Pietro All right.
Geoffrey Thank you.

Geoffrey holds out his hand and Pietro takes it. Geoffrey hangs on and "explores" Pietro

You're overweight.
Pietro Ish.
Geoffrey No taller than me.
Pietro I am.
Geoffrey Ish. Thinning?
Pietro Ish. Ish.
Geoffrey She'll like that.
Pietro She already does.

The Lights fade

The stools are removed and the main set converted back to the treatment room

The Lights come up on Alice and Geoffrey

Alice is leaving

Alice I do love you, you know.
Geoffrey I love you. But you can close now.
Alice What?
Geoffrey The information bureau.

Alice Oh.

Geoffrey And anyway, I've been invited over for pasta with basil and walnut sauce. So I'll see you.

Alice Geoffrey …

Geoffrey I'll be fine. You know I'll be fine. Especially knowing that you're happy.

Alice I'll miss you so much.

Geoffrey You won't. You've got a lot of Peter Clemenson to work on.

Alice Geoffrey …

Geoffrey What?

Alice You are noble, do you know that?

Geoffrey The advantage of being blind is that you can see some things very clearly.

Alice kisses Geoffrey

(*Feeling his watch*) I've got a half-past four appointment.

Alice Who is it?

Geoffrey Can't remember. I'll know soon enough.

Alice Oh, Geoffrey …

Geoffrey Stop Geoffreying me. Anton will come and tape my appointments for me. Though he seems to go to a lot of aerobics classes now. And he's signed on for badminton, softball and squash.

Alice (*looking at the apppointments diary*) It's Nicola.

Pause

Her "l" goes up a long way.

Geoffrey Sorry?

Alice Her "l". The loop goes very high. Bumps into the line above.

Geoffrey Does it?

The doorbell rings

Let her in on your way out then.

Alice turns to leave

I'll miss you too, Alice.

Alice exits

Nicola enters

Nicola Hallo, Geoffrey.
Geoffrey My wife has left me.
Nicola How do you feel about that?
Geoffrey You can imagine.
Nicola Yes.
Geoffrey And all because of a letter.
Nicola A letter?
Geoffrey An anonymous letter.
Nicola From somebody who believes in fair play?
Geoffrey From somebody with very tall "l"s.
Nicola Really?
Geoffrey How's business?
Nicola I've negotiated. Fifty per cent.
Geoffrey How do you feel about that?

Nicola jingles some car keys in front of Geoffrey

Nicola Drives like a dream.
Geoffrey And him?
Nicola He'll replace me with a lorry.
Geoffrey Where are you?
Nicola Here.

Nicola moves to Geoffrey and they enfold each other in a hungry kiss

The Lights fade

FURNITURE AND PROPERTY LIST

On stage: Chair with extending footrest, set reclining. *On it*: cosy white
    towel or similar
    Low stool
    Desk. *On it*: computer (practical), dictaphone, telephone,
    diary, pen, CD remote control
    Typing chair
    Plants

Off stage: Box containing roller-skate wheels (**Anton**)
    Shopping bag, unopened letters including one from overseas
    (**Alice**)

Personal: **Geoffrey**: watch (worn throughout)
    Nicola: car keys

During scene change p. 16:

Re-set: Reclining chair to upright position

Set: Clipboard on desk

Strike: Chair cover

During scene change p. 24:

Set: Two stools

During scene change p. 28:

Re-set: Chair to reclining position, with cover

Strike: Two stools

LIGHTING PLOT

Practical fittings required: computer monitor
Three interiors

To open: Darkness

Cue 1	When ready *Bring up general interior lighting on* *treatment room setting; dim computer glow*	(Page 1)
Cue 2	**Alice** exits *Fade lights to evening setting with mellow light* *and brighten glow from computer monitor*	(Page 9)
Cue 3	**Alice** switches on the main light *Bring up general interior lighting on* *treatment room setting; dim computer glow*	(Page 9)
Cue 4	**Alice** exits *Fade all lights*	(Page 16)
Cue 5	When ready *Bring up general interior lights on* *leisure centre setting; dim computer glow*	(Page 16)
Cue 6	**Peter**, **Anton** and **Amaryllis** exit *Fade all lights*	(Page 24)
Cue 7	When ready *Bring up lights on two stools*	(Page 24)
Cue 8	**Pietro**: "She already does." *Fade lights*	(Page 28)
Cue 9	When ready *Bring up general interior lighting on* *treatment room setting; dim computer glow*	(Page 28)
Cue 10	**Nicola** enfolds **Geoffrey** *Fade all lights*	(Page 30)

EFFECTS PLOT